TABLE OF CONTENTS

The Papal Palace, circa 1660
Laincel album
Calvet Museum, Avignon

"OLD AVIGNON"

1

Avignon in the first centuries

The rock of the Doms, a natural refuge overlooking the Rhone, was inhabited during the Neolithic age. Gradually, the population expanded along the south-west slope. Avignon, the city of the Cavares, owed its development to a geographic position whose strategic importance was noted by the Romans. From the 4th century, Christianity took root outside the walls. Faced with the threat of barbarian invasions, the city abandoned the Roman fortifications and fell back on the Rock.

Abandoned to the Moors, Charles Martel reconquered it twice, in 737 and 739. In the 10th century, the city was part of the kingdom of Arles and was ruled by a count, living in the castrum of the Rock. In the eleventh century, the cathedral of Notre-Dame-des-Doms was rebuilt. The old Christian basilica outside of the walls became the abbey of Saint-Ruf and soon became a renowned school of sculpture. The development of the city encouraged the rise of an urban aristocracy. The city, now the joint property of three counts, proclaimed itself a free town at the beginning of the 12th century. Many strong-houses were built with their towers dominating the city. During this period of exceptional prosperity, the Saint Benezet bridge was built across the Rhone, connecting the two banks of the river. The Romanesque city covered the same area as the old Roman-occupied area and new protective fortifications were built, surrounding the recently founded churches.

In 1226, the Avignonnais, having sided with the count of Toulouse, refused passage to Louis VIII during the crusade against the Albigenses. After a siege of three months, they surrendered and suffered the hard conditions of defeat : demolition of the ramparts, from the bridge to the fourth arch, destruction of

2

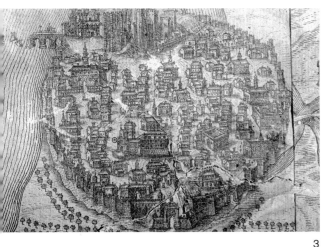

3

4

At the beginning of the 14th century

three hundred strong-houses, and the appointment of an ultramontane bishop. In spite of this harsh treatment, the city rose from its ruins and the mendicant orders took root outside the partly rebuilt walls. The Hospitaler and Templar knights founded their headquarters there.

It was in this peaceful context that the little city's destiny took a sudden shift when the papacy installed its court there. By setting up residence there, Clement V had no idea of the destiny he was preparing for Avignon. The city belonged to Charles of Anjou, King of Jerusalem and Sicily, and bordered on the Comtat Venaissin, a papal possession since 1274. Therefore, the pope could flee troubles in Italy and escape the influence of the king of France in a safe refuge. However, it was Clement's successor John XXII and his munificence that brought the first changes to the urban landscape. Benedict XII and Clement VI

5

completed his work by the construction of the Apostolic Palace. Many cardinalice palaces were built and all forms of art were used for the embellishment of these residences and religious edifices.

The city then overflowed from the Romanesque enclosure. Avignon became a spectacular and disorderly sprawl of houses along badly paved and filthy streets. The impressions of the poet Petrarch when he discovered the city are significant: "the filthiest of cities, horribly windy, badly constructed, no conveniences, a hell for the living". Petrarch adds that the city was the "most odoriferous on earth". Was there some Latin exaggeration in these words ?

1 - Drawing on parchment, by Nicholas d'Ypres (1514), Avignon and the palace under the legation of Cardinal Clermont Lodeve (District archives).
2 - Figurine sculpted in bone in the Old Avignon Museum, discovered in the Lower Treasury hall.
3 - Old Avignon, engraving by Greuther Matthaus (1564-1638) reconstruction of the city in the 12th century?
4 - Map of Avignon, the Rhone and the Durance. Drawing and engraving by Louis David in 1696.
5 - Seal of Charles of Anjou, Count of Provence (District archives)

The Comtat Venaissin

1

1 - Map of the Comtat Venaissin
(District archives)

Detail from the map of Avignon,
featuring the rock of Doms
The so-called "Map with
characters" 1572

A highly coveted region over the years, the Comtat's borders varied with history. Bordered by Orange to the north, the land of Apt to the east, Cavaillon and Chateaurenard to the south and the Rhone to the west, the Comtat area was Roman land until 476. In the 6th century, the bishop of Carpentras left his city and moved to Venasque (the source of the Comtat Venaissin's name).

Until the 14th century, Pernes-les-Fontaines was the capital of the Comtat Venaissin. The Comtat was made a part of the county of Provence in 993, and was divided once again in 1125, when the land north of the Durance was ceded to the count of Toulouse.

The year 1229 saw the defeat of the Albigenses and the Comtat was then recovered from the defeated count Raymond VII. The Comtat lands were given to Pope Gregory X by Philip the Bold in 1274 ; at that time the lands were christened "Comtat Venaissin".

In 1320, the Comtat could be proud of its institutions. Its capital, Carpentras, was home to the administration and courts. In addition to its independent status, the Comtat was also famous for its fertile alluvial plains, perfect for agriculture.

The rock of Doms

Its position, which provides a breathtaking panoramic view, has made the rock a place of refuge since prehistoric times. In the second century, the Romans built a castrum on this defensive site, while the Roman town was established south-west of the rock. The castrum was converted into a castle during the 11th century, which then became the residence of the counts of Provence. But from the 4th century on, the bishop of Avignon is said to have established his residence there, on the promontory overlooking the Rhone. The rock, and the future cathedral, took their names from the area (de domo episcopali). In the 13th century, the Avignon township held its grand assemblies at the foot of Saint Anne's steps.

The Rhone

Without a doubt a strong influence on Avignon's development, the unpredictable Rhone river opened the city to the commercial routes between the Mediterranean and the Northern lands. From the Alps, Italy or Spain, all roads at the time seemed to pass through Avignon. Between 1177 and 1185, the construction of the Benezet bridge permitted further expansion of the city. Since Arles had lost its ancient port, Avignon was the very first chance to cross the river since the Mediterranean coast. In the 13th century, Avignon and Marseilles had steady trade relations. Through the port of Aigues-Mortes, seagoing ships sailed up to Arles and, depending on their draft, up to the rock of Doms. In the south-west of the city, the bend of the river was more pronounced than it is today and its banks were home to all sorts of activities. The main port, under the Benezet bridge, was the successor to the port of the Periers (stonecutters). Upstream from the rock, the wood shipped by the river was unloaded. In the 14th century, the illustrious figures that came to visit the popes in Avignon travelled on the Rhône.

1

How the Popes came to settle in Avignon

1 - Avignon, illumination early
15th century,
(District Archives)

2 - Lead locket
found in one of the rooms of
the Lower Treasury Hall of the
Papal Palace

At the dawning of the 14th century, the papacy was experiencing a great many, mainly political, problems. Complex circumstances caused it to take temporary residence in Avignon. In Italy, civil war pitched the Guelphs, who were the Pope's allies, against the Ghibelines, who sided with the Emperor, and created a climate of insecurity that prevented the Supreme Pontiff from living in Rome and from governing the Holy See states. Throughout the 13th century, the Pope and his court, the Curia, were constantly on the move and rarely in Rome. They usually took up residence in the cities of their Italian states. Philip the Fair, King of France, refused to recognise the Pope's temporal supremacy. After the attack on Pope Boniface VIII in his Anagni palace in 1303, the king once again put the papacy to the test by forcing Clement V to suppress the Knights Templar. The choice of Avignon as a temporary papal residence was no coincidence. The city belonged to the Count of Provence, Charles II of Anjou, King of Naples and Sicily who, as such, was vassal to the Pope, to whom he lent his support. Furthermore, Avignon was close to the Comtat Venaissin, which had been a church possession since the late 13th century, and which now largely comprises the present departement of Vaucluse. This territory, which lies at the meeting point of the Rhone and Durance rivers, bordered the kingdom of France to which it was linked by the famous Benezet Bridge and was at peace and stable. It was also ideally situated at the heart of Christian Europe, between France, Spain and Italy, and was a fiefdom of the Holy Roman Empire.

Papal Avignon, overpopulation and change

When the popes moved into Avignon, the papal court required housing for itself and for cardinals with their retinues, in addition to a mob of cosmopolitan merchants. Avignon, which had only 6000 people at the beginning of the century, swelled to 30,000 under Clement VI.

Convents and monasteries were insufficient to house the members of the Curia. To recover housing, the papal administration bought out the occupants of the houses in town. Pope Benedict XII, realising the abusive behaviour of certain cardinals, enacted laws to protect the people and property owners. Population movements outside the walls were encouraged and volunteers moving to the country were exempted from papal taxes. Villages developed outside of the 12th century enclosure. A new habitat of wood structures and cob walls developed. The urban landscape and traffic were in upheaval. Some cardinals fenced in their residences (cancels) and even closed off streets and built catwalks to pass over them. This overcrowded promiscuous setting was ideal ground for the spread of fires and epidemics. The plague, which ravaged the city several times, brought a sad solution to overpopulation. The epidemic of 1348, it is believed, decimated half the population of Avignon.

A cultural and artistic cross-roads

The arrival of the popes in Avignon and the population flow which followed it deeply changed the urban landscape. While the popes enlarged their residence, the bishop built the new bishop's palace, now known as the Small Palace.

The cardinals moved into luxurious accommodations the "livrées cardinalices" of which the Ceccano today remains a magnificent example. Gradually the Gothic style replaced the Romanesque, the more modest churches and convents were enlarged or rebuilt. Lords and burghers, merchants and bankers competed in luxury, symbolising their status and rank in Avignon society. At the time, the city was a permanent construction site and the Pope's palace was the largest project of the century. The architects (Pierre Poisson, Jean de Louvres...) and painters (Pierre du Puy, Jean Dalbon and Matteo Giovannetti...) worked on the construction and decoration of the Popes' Palace

The finest artisans, glassmakers, jewellers, weavers, carpetmakers rushed to the city for orders. This mix of styles, which the Flemish and the Italians dominated gave rise to the school of Avignon. An exceptional melting pot for all artistic expression, Avignon was a true cultural capital. Rich and mindful of their prestige, the popes were also generous patrons and attracted many scientists and scholars. They did not neglect letters and the pontifical library acquired magnificent illuminated manuscripts. 2650 volumes were counted at the departure of the popes from Avignon. The poet Petrarch, although hostile to the "exile" of the papacy, was honoured in the palace where he had erudite friends among the cardinals. He also met Laure de Noves, object of his passion, in the church of the nuns of Saint Claire. In 1303, the university, which already had a school of arts and medicine, created a school of law which soon welcomed the most reputed jurists of the time. In the first half of the 14th century, Avignon flourished economically and culturally.

The fortifications

From the rock of Doms, the city has been protected by ramparts throughout history.

Rectangular under the Romans, then restricted to the foot of the rock in the early Middle Ages, the ramparts were rebuilt in the 12th century over the outline of the old Roman fort. They consisted of two walls protected by moats.

Victorious in the siege of the city in 1226, the King of France ordered their destruction. One century later, deprived of its fortifications, the rich papal city was an ideal target for plunderers and mercenaries freed by truces in the Hundred-Years War. Pope Innocent VI hurriedly undertook the construction of new fortifications, encompassing the new townships. Completed in 1376 under the reign of Gregory XI, the ramparts included 35 defensive towers and 4330 meters long were to a height they rose of eight meters over the moats, which have since been filled in.

Seven gates closed by drawbridges provided access to the enclosure punctuated by crenelated towers with merlons and connected by walls. The citizens of Avignon accepted these expensive works not only because they deterred possible attackers but also because they protected against frequent flooding by the Rhone (there were about forty floods during the 13th century).

2

1

1 - Portraits of the Avignon popes imagined by Henry Serrur, from 1839 to 1840: Clement V, John XXII, Benedict XII, Clement VI, Innocent VI, Urban V, Gregory XI, Clement VII, Benedict XIII.

All the members of the Pontifical Court were clerics, with the exception of those who only resided there infrequently. They held various administrative, diplomatic or domestic functions, depending on which religious order they belonged to.

The Pope's close entourage consisted first and foremost of immediate family, chaplains, doctors, stewards, and attendants called cubiculars. Secondly, the **Sacred College**, headed by the Cardinal Chamberlain, consisted entirely of cardinals. The College received the revenue earmarked for the cardinals from the Apostolic Chamber. They met in Consistory with the Pope, but lived outside the palace in private mansions, or "liveries", which also included a substantial household. A cardinal's chaplains, secretaries, squires and servants were called his familia, and could be as many as 50 in number.

Then came the Roman Church's central administration, which was divided into four institutions, the main instruments of its government :

The **Apostolic Chamber**, the financial service which took in taxes from the entire Christian world ;

2

The **Chancellery**, the office which dispatched the pontifical correspondence and dealt with the allocation of ecclesiastic privileges ;

The **legal administration** with various courts, including the Court of the Rota, which judged ecclesiastic privilege cases;

And lastly, the **Penitentiary**, the spiritual tribunal which, in the Pope's name, granted canonical dispensatioris and levied punishments and censures.

There were also the various services such as the guard of honour services, which escorted the Pope on visits, ensured his protection and upheld order inside the palace. These guards were horsemen, noble squires, porters and sergeants-at-arms, numbering some one to two hundred men, depending on the Pope.

Then came the palace's four offices, the domestic services : kitchen, pantry, bottle-room and blacksmith. They were responsible for food and provisions for the pontifical court in the palace and when it travelled. Every day, they served over 300 meals and distributed bread and wine to 800 of the poor. Minor personnel and workhands were responsible for the upkeep of the palace and gardens.

Everything revolved around the Pope and his sacred person. Liturgical life affected all aspects of existence at the palace. From the Chamberlain to the lowest ranking sergeant, all attended the permanent offices said by the commensal chaplains at different times of the day.

2 - Pope Clement V holding consistory (District archives).

3 - Departure of Clement V for Rome in 1367 (manuscript in the Avignon city library).

The seven French popes : "captives of Babylon"

All the Avignon popes considered their stay in Avignon temporary. Exceptional, essentially political circumstances forced them to live there for almost a century. Clement V (1305-1314) an itinerant pope, resided in the Dominican convent of Avignon and in other papal residences in the Comtat.

John XXII (1316-1334) moved into the bishop's palace that he was familiar with since he had been bishop of Avignon. He embellished this stronghouse located where the Old Palace now stands. A great builder, John XXII also renovated the papal residences in the Comtat and built a luxurious summer house on the banks of the Sorgue river. Organiser of papal revenues, he increased the papal treasure. He died at the age of 90. Benedict XII (1334-1342) a former Cistercian monk, elected after two years of vacancy, bought the old bishop's palace transformed by John XXII. Using the riches accumulated by his predecessor, he had Pierre Poisson build a fortified and large residence, of sober architecture. This pope also restored order to the papal court, punishing abuses by his officials and the secular clergy. Like his predecessor, he increased taxes for

the papal treasury. When he died in 1342, his palace, the Old Palace, was almost completed. Clement VI (1342-1352) was favoured by the king of France when elected. A well-educated aristocrat, noted theologian and fine orator, he was a liberal and generous patron of the arts. A munificent ruler, he decided to enlarge the palace. Jean de Louvre built the New Palace, giving the edifice its gothic elegance and its final appearance. Clement VI called upon Matteo Giovanetti to decorate. Clement VI's new palace had been completed just one year when he died, after having bought the city of Avignon from Queen Jeanne in 1348. Innocent VI (1352-1362) was determined to reconquer the papal lands in Italy. He consolidated the work of Clement VI and undertook construction of new ramparts to protect the city. Urban V (1362-1370) beautified the gardens and built the Roma there in 1367. He left for Rome in 1367 but the perils of the eternal city led him to return to Avignon in 1370, where he died a few months after his return. Gregory XI (1370-1378) succeeded in restoring the Holy See to Rome in 1376. His death, two years later, 3 marked the end of the line of French popes.

The schism

Clement VII and Benedict XII are considered schismatic by the Church. Their names were subsequently used by other popes.

Gathered in Rome in 1378 upon the death of Gregory XII, the sacred college was divided. Under popular pressure, the Italian cardinals elected Urban VI, an Italian pope. But the 13 French cardinals disputed the conditions of the election. They chose Robert of Geneva as Pope Clement VII. A schism was declared which lasted 40 years. The death of Urban VI in Rome, then that of Clement VII, did not end the schism. The sacred colleges in Rome and Avignon again elected two new popes.

Gregory XII was elected in Rome in 1402. Benedict XIII, Pedro de Luna, from a noble family of Aragon, was elected in Avignon in 1394. The two popes mutually excommunicated each

other. A council met in 1409 in Pisa and deposed both popes and designated a third, Alexander V, succeeded by John XXIII in 1410. There were now three popes. The Council of Constance in 1414 affirmed the supremacy of council decisions over the will of the pope and obtained the abdication of Gregory XII and of John XXIII then ordered the election of Martin V two years later. The schism was over. However, Benedict XIII refused to abdicate. Abandoned by the French cardinals who asked him to capitulate, he withdrew into his besieged palace, defying the revolt of the people of Avignon and the assaults of Geoffrey de Boucicaut, mercenary serving the king of France. He fled one night in 1403. Exiled in Spain, Benedict XIII died forgotten in 1423, aged 94, still convinced he was the legitimate pope.

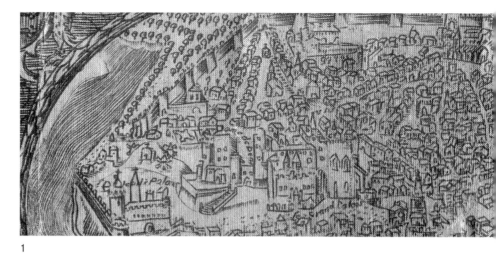

1

The largest gothic palace in Europe

An impressive building, the palace is described by Froissart in his Chronicles as the "most beautiful and powerful house in the world". This admiration is justified ; with its thick walls, its towers rising to more than 50 meters high, its huge rooms, the marvellous painted decoration of the chapels and apartments, the Papal Palace reflects the luxury and cultural influence of the papal court: a residence worthy of the pope, first prince of Christendom. It is the work of two popes : Benedict XII, who built the Old Palace, and Clement VI who built the New Palace. Over the palace of John XXII, Benedict XII had a second huge and powerful apostolic residence erected between 1335 and 1342. As of 1343, Clement VI ordered the addition of the south and west wings. This work reflected a new spirit in architecture and decoration. In the New Palace there are intersecting ribs and vaults and new original shapes ; windows and doors feature mouldings and sculptures, wider staircases...

1- Supposed representation of the bishop's palace, detail (Old Avignon Museum).
2 - Drawing, from an engraving, Bibliotheque nationale

2

1   2   3

The palace of John XXII

After his election, on 7 August 1316, Pope John XXII, who had been bishop of Avignon from 1310 to 1313, moved into his former residence, the bishop's palace. Until his death, John XXII tried to enlarge and transform this edifice into a papal residence.

South of Notre-Dame-des-Doms, the bishop's palace was arranged around a cloister which was trapezoidal in shape due to the irregular forms of the rock. John XXII, hoping to enlarge the palace, bought the neighbouring houses to demolish them so as to enlarge the Consistory wing to the south: this wing included the apartments of the Treasurer, the Chamberlain, and the Great Treasury. The modified building was a foretaste of the approximate layout of the future palace of Benedict XII. All that remains of the palace of John XXII are traces of the Audience room that the pope had built in a building parallel to the palace, which are visible in the Honour Courtyard.

1 - Benedict XII by Paul of Sienna (1341), moulding, north sacristy.
2 - The Pope's tower, first construction by Benedict XII.
3 - Courtyard of honour (Cour d'Honneur),
vestiges of the Audience of John XXII, well.
4 - Papal bull by Innocent IV (1243-1254).

4

THE POPES' PALACE

OLD PALACE

TROUILLAS TOWER

CAMPANE TOWER

KITCHEN
TOWER

A

D

12

NOTRE-DAME-
DES-DOMS

11

10

8

B

C

21

E

20

THE ANGLE
TOWER

1

THE CHAMPEAUX GATE

2

A - CHAPEL OF BENEDICT XII
B - THE FAMILIARS' WING
C - CONCLAVE WING
D - CONSISTORY WING
E - GRAND DIGNITARIES WING
F - GRAND CHAPEL

This illustration of the Popes' Palace shows the differences in construction of the palace of Benedict XII or Old Palace, and that of his successor Clement VI, called the New Palace.

The numbering refers to the itinerary of the audio-guided tour.

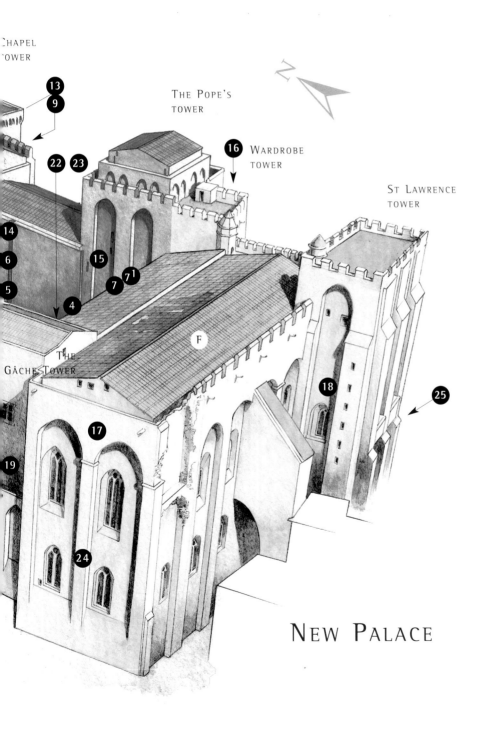

CHAPEL TOWER

THE POPE'S TOWER

WARDROBE TOWER

ST LAWRENCE TOWER

THE GÂCHE TOWER

NEW PALACE

The Builders of the Old Palace

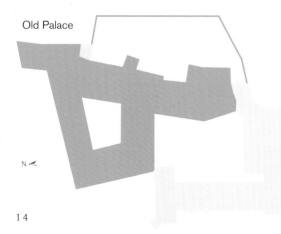

1

In 1340, the Familiars' wing, now the Campane tower, the cloister galleries and the outdoor staircase leading to the Papal Chapel were all built above the location of the apartments of John XXII. In the Audience square, a crenelated rampart was built to reinforce the "Porte Majeure" (Main Gate). Within seven years, Pierre Poisson's successive projects had covered almost a hectare and employed many workers. In May 1337, there were 800 workers on the palace site.

The construction of the imposing Trouillas tower, designed to ensure the defence of the north-east of the palace went on from 1341 to 1346. Benedict XII did not live to see his achievement. He died in April 1342, his project nearly completed after seven years of rule : a majestic palace with the external appearance of a fortress, with huge rooms to which wood ceilings and frames bestowed a special character.

Benedict XII and Pierre Poisson

2

Benedict XII bought the bishop's palace transformed by John XXII and began work in 1335. A native of Mirepoix, Pierre Poisson first received the honorific title of squire before being chosen as papal architect and master of works and edifices. Work began with the construction of the Pope's tower, a 46-meter high fortified tower with thick walls designed to house the treasury at its base and the new papal apartments. He enlarged St. Stephen's church, which became the papal chapel (renamed chapel of Benedict XII). The Conclave wing, the private apartments wing (today destroyed), the Study tower, the Consistory and the Great Tinel, the Chapels tower, the Latrines tower, the kitchens and the garden rampart were all built in 1337.

Construction materials

In addition to the various trades, fustiers (carpenters), quarrymen and labourers, the successive building projects at the palace involved the transport of huge amounts of materials.

The stones required for the structural work were taken from the quarries in nearby Villeneuve-les-Avignon. The pavement slabs came from Caromb or from the Comtat's quarries. For the sculpted decors or the sections exposed to weather, rugged white Orgon limestone was preferred to fragile sandstone (known as "pierre du midi") which the walls were made of. The gypsum lodes of the Isle-sur-Sorgue provided plaster while tiles provided came from Chateauneuf-Calcernier. The wood for frames and ceilings came from Savoy (larch), Vivarais (oak), usually lashed into huge floating rafts and transported by the Rhone.

Old Palace

New Palace

N

3   4

Clement VI and Jean de Louvres

5

1 - The Chapels Tower,
Old Palace
2 - Benedict XII
(District Archives)
3 - The Angle Tower,
New Palace
4 - Coat of Arms of Clement VI,
Champeaux gate
5 - Clement VI
(District Archives)

The son of a noble family, Clement VI was a munificent prince. Elected on 7 May 1342, he decided that summer to build a new palace. The construction was entrusted to Jean de Louvres, master mason, from Parisis. Little is known of the man except that he was appointed master of papal works and sergeant at arms and that he remained in the service of Clement VI until his death in 1357. In the summer of 1342, construction started on the Wardrobe tower against the south wall and the Kitchens tower was built between the garden rampart and the Latrine tower. After the first section was completed in 1343, the pope decided to finish the Trouillas tower. In 1344, stones were cut to lay the foundations of the Grand Audience hall (May 1345). The Great Chapel project began at the end of 1346, ending only in 1351, slowed down by the epidemic of plague in 1348. Construction continued through 1351 : the Great Promenade, the Peyrolerie gate, the La Gache gate and the Grand Dignitaries Wing (completed in 1347). On the city side, the Champeaux Gate, cut in the new façade, marked the main entrance. The west wing attached to Benedict XII's palace delimited the new enclosed area of the Courtyard of Honour. Work on the south wing had been completed for one year when Clement VI died on 6 December, 1352. With Clement VI, gothic elegance entered the palace. Intersecting ribs abound: sculptures, "rib bases", mouldings decorate the stone. The walls are covered with magnificent frescoes while the furnishings are enriched with sumptuous hangings.

Completing the works

The cost of the new palace had emptied the financial reserves of the Holy See when Innocent VI was elected in 1352. Clement VI's successors had to be content with completing the work begun and making limited transformations. In 1353, the La Gache tower was raised, the south wing reinforced by the construction of the St. Lawrence tower, completed in 1356. The following year, the flying buttress of the la Peyrolerie gate lent support to the Great Chapel. To save his strength, Innocent VI, in poor health, connected the Little Tinel and the North Sacristy by a bridge which was destroyed in 1811. In 1364, Urban V ordered the building of La Roma, a multi-storey gallery abutting on the Study Tower, destroyed by the military in 1837.

1

2

Paintings, fragments of history

Among the many painters who decorated the palace only three received the title of "Master" : Pierre du Puy under John XXII ; Jean Dalbon under Benedict XII, Matteo Giovanetti under Clement VI. The masters supervised teams of painters and the palace book show the names of many unknown artists.

To transform the bishop's palace into an apostolic residence, John XXII called upon many painters from Toulouse and the south working under the supervision of Master Pierre du Puy. There remains nothing of these first painted decors except a few traces which are legible only to specialists. Most of the painters working on the successive projects of the palace came from Italy. But it is a Frenchman, Jean Dalbon, whose name remains linked to that of Benedict XII ; the pope entrusted him with the decoration of his rooms and his studium. Robin de Romans, another Frenchman, is said to have painted the north wall of the Benedict XII's room and the account books also mention a certain Hugo... Many questions remain.

Only a part of the extraordinary work of Matteo Giovannetti, painter to Pope Clement VI, has reached us today. All of his preserved painted decors are located in the section of the monument open to the public. In the Wardrobe tower, the superb friezes decorating the ceilings of the Upper Wardrobe are said to be the work of Bernard Escot and Pierre de Castres.

On the north wall of the guest's apartments in Benedict XII's palace, part of a trompe-l'oeil decor was discovered with a fine twisted column supporting an arcature and balustrade, on a background spangled with six-pointed stars.

3

4

5

6

Of the 18th-century decors done at the time of the vice-legates, there remain military inspired "grisaille" motifs in the Small Audience hall, wich was transformed into an arsenal at the time. Other 18th century decoration includes the south Guards room and the paintings of the Vestry, a chapel at the time. Elsewhere in the palace only traces remain. Most of the painted decors suffered over the centuries : fires, vandalism, depredations...In 1413, a fire ravaged the Consistory wing...At the end of the 18th century, the Saint Martial chapel was converted into a lead foundry...

In the 19th century, when the palace was used as a barracks, Prosper Merimee was outraged by soldiers selling fragments of frescoes from the palace. The restorations carried out at the beginning of the century were often harmful to their preservation...

With joint support from the European Community, the city and the French government, an extraordinary effort has been undertaken today to restore the frescoes of Saint Martial chapel.

1 - Frescoes of Saint John chapel, damaged by military engineers
2 - The Stag Room, ceiling and frieze
3 - 5 - Frescoes, Guest apartments, Convention Centre
4 - Fresco, Upper Wardrobe

7

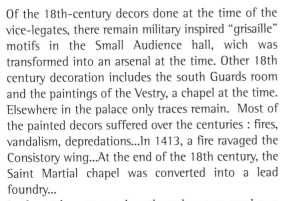

8

6 - Fragment of sinopia, Saint Michael chapel
7 - Decor, window splay, Pope's room
8 - Detail of a restored fragment of the fresco, Old Chamberlain's Chamber

MATTEO GIOVANNETTI

Detail of the frescoes, Saint-
John Chapel,
The Feast of Herod,
Salome presenting the head
of John the Baptist to
Herodias.

Matteo Giovanetti was an ecclesiastic born around 1300. Although a native of Viterbo, he was an artist in the Sienna tradition and indeed one of its most inventive proponents. His name first appeared in account ledgers in 1343 and he was awarded the title of painter to the Pope in 1346. As master painter and chief craftsman, he played a major part in the Palace's pictorial decoration.

Unfortunately, only three complete works have survived the ravages of time and man : Saint John's Chapel, Saint Martial's Chapel and an arch in the Great Audience Hall. The works which have disappeared are the decorations of Saint Michael's Chapel, the Consistory, La Roma (the building constructed by Urban V), the decoration of the Great Audience Hall, a Last Judgement and a Calvary. Matteo Giovanetti's long stay at the Pontifical Court gave him the freedom

he needed to develop his own style, which owed much to Simone Martini and to the Sienese tradition.

His talents as a storyteller were greatly admired, as was his lively poetic imagination, which ranged from the anecdotal in Saint Martial's Chapel to mystic grandeur in Saint John's Chapel. His originality lay first and foremost in his extremely fine eye for the interplay of perspectives - he created a great many interior scenes and representations of architecture in trompe-l'oeil, which are wall paintings giving the illusion of three dimensions. While many artists of the period painted faces according to convention, Matteo Giovanetti was a true portrait painter. The rich decoration and elegant clothing of his figures attest to the Pontifical Court's lavish way of life.

He was without a doubt the most prominent of all the artists who worked at the palace.

Fresco techniques

Fresco techniques, which had already been used in Antiquity, experienced a genuine revival in Italy during the 13th century and flourished throughout the 14th and 15th centuries. The name comes from the Italian fresco which means fresh, because the technique consists in painting on wet mortar.

First, the brick or stone wall on which the fresco is to be painted is prepared by applying three fine layers of lime mortar. The first layer is used to smooth out the facing, the second layer, the arricio receives the sinopia which is a sketch of the future work done with iron oxide from Sinope, a town on the Black Sea. The final layer, the intonaco, receives the colour pigments. Depending on the season and climate, the artist has approximately seven hours , the length of time the mortar stays wet, to complete the fresco. Plaster is only applied to the surface area that can be treated during those few hours. The speed of the technique requires great skill. As it dries, the lime in the mortar crystallises and fixes the pigments indelibly on the surface, which has by then become hard and very solid. Reworkings and afterthoughts, which are painted dry or "a secco", are much more fragile. The drawing can be done from a sketch or a stencil, where the outline is traced using a toothed wheel. A gauze pad is used to apply charcoal powder through the perforations in the overlay, this transferring the drawing to the wall. A stiletto can also be used to follow the outlines by making incisions in the wet plaster.

A PAINTER DURING THE TIME OF THE POPES SIMONE MARTINI

Sinopia uncovered during the removal of the frescoes of the porch of the Notre-Dame-des-Doms Cathedral The Virgin and Child.

The frescoes painted by Simone Martini, who decorated the porch of Notre Dame des Doms Cathedral, are on display on the West wall of the Consistory Hall.

Simone Martini, a renowned artist who was famed for his paintings of the life of Saint Martin in the lower Church of Saint Francis in Assisi, was born in Siena in 1284. He went to Avignon in 1340 at the invitation of Cardinal Stefane. The great Italian prelate was a patron of the arts who had already commissioned works from Giotto for Saint Peter's in Rome.

Simone Martini's formal compositions and his idealised treatment of the holy figures are tempered by poetic sensitivity. During, the last four years of his life, this great friend of Petrarch played a major part in the development of Provençal culture, despite his brief stay there.

1 THE GUARDS' ROOM

2 THE SMALL AUDIENCE HA

It was in this room, located on the right under the Champeaux doorway, that the guards responsible for watching the main gate of the palace were stationed. Most admirable are the bases of the ribs (in particular the one consisting of seven characters), the intersecting ribs and the lovely proportions. The frescoes decorating the walls were added at the beginning of the 17th century when the vice-legates were living in the palace. On the north wall, a large allegorical painting shows the pope flanked by two children personifying Justice, on the left, Prudence on the right. Facing it, among a set of coats of arms, may be seen the golden emblematic bees of the family of Urban VIII, the Barberini family.

The Small Audience Hall was a court linked to the Chancellery, the department that dealt with petitions and disputes raised by apostolic letters.
The auditor judged the most complex cases and sat on a small podium of three steps, situated in the northern part of the hall.
This magnificently vaulted hall, with two uneven intersecting ribs, boasts a handsome set of carved capitals. In the east, a recess containing a tabernacle and a piscina - a stone basin for draining water used in the mass - was used as an oratory.
In the early 17th century, during the vice-legateship period, the Small Audience Hall was turned into an arsenal. The "grisaille" decor of the vault dates from this time, and depicts military trophies, standards and banners which bear mottoes on the theme of war and peace.

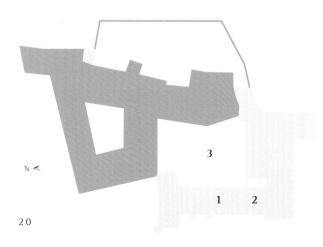

N

3

1   2

3 THE HONOUR COURTYARD

The Popes' Palace is primarily the result of two palaces being joined together : the Old Palace, built on the East and North sides by Benedict XII, and the New Palace, built by his successor Clement VI, on the South and West sides. When Benedict XII died in 1342, Clement VI commenced the expansion of his predecessor's residence and acquired the buildings to the South of the Old Palace for demolition. The new buildings would form a square : the Cour d'Honneur or Courtyard of Honour.

Let us now look North-eastwards, at the façades of the Old Palace.

The tallest tower, the Pope's Tower or Angel Tower, built in 1335, has all the characteristics of a keep : the height, the buttresses which punctuate the walls, the blind first storeys and, on top, the crenellations and machicolations and small sparsely interspersed embrasures.

In front of the ivy-covered façade, a major building long since disappeared housed some of the Pope's private apartments. It was linked to the southern wing by a small bridge, built during Pope Innocent VI's reign.

Access to the Old Palace was originally through a fortified entrance known as the Porte Majeure or Main Gate. The entrance was bored through one of the ramparts running, parallel to the façade of the South Wing. All that is left of it today is part of a wall to the West, adorning the small tower known as Cardinal Blanc's tower. On the East side, this rampart abuts onto the building which houses the private apartments.

If you now turn to face southwards, you will see that the façade of the New Palace has wider and more numerous windows. There are no buttresses. Construction work on the New Palace began in 1342 with the Wardrobe Tower, next to the Pope's Tower.

Work on the South Wing started in 1345 with the Great Audience Hall and the Great Chapel that is directly above it, and was completed in 1351. On the south-west side of this building, arcading opens onto a stepped portico which also served as a mounting block for horsemen. In the corner, the porch provides access to the Great Audience Hall and the landing of a monumental staircase, which is lit by the windows visible in this façade.

The Pope would give his triple blessing from the Indulgence Window. Work on the West Wing, called the Grand Dignitaries Wing, also commenced in 1345 and was completed two years later. This low-slung elongated building forms the west façade of the New Palace. The Champeaux Gate is built into it and boasts a suspended keystone, the only one of its kind in the Palace.

There are two secondary gates where the two palaces meet: the Notre-Dame Gate, on the north-west side, was used for processions and when the Holy Father left the palace, as it opened onto the road leading to the cathedral. The Peyrolerie Gate, on the south-east side, was used to reach the far side of the palace.

4 The Lower Treasury Hall

The Lower Treasury Hall is on the second of the Pope's Tower six floors and housed all that was precious to the Holy See. This room's arched ceiling is divided up into four compartments with intersecting ribs descending onto a central column. On the wall side, the ribs descend onto pyramid-shaped imposts.

The Treasury's wealth varied from Pope to Pope. John XXII contributed heavily to its growth. However, Clement VI's work on the New Palace, and the wars waged by Innocent VI in Italy, eroded the Treasure. After Urban V, the deficit became permanent. The Treasury could only meet its expenditures by borrowing.

It was in the masonry hiding places beneath the slabs of the Lower Treasury that bags of money, the finest gold pieces and gold and silverware, were kept. In 1348, Clement VI's tableware weighed around 196 kg and comprised all manner of utensils: trays, vessels, lidded cups, ewers, vermeil or silver-gilt flasks and the like. Church ornaments, archives, property deeds and accounting ledgers were also stored there. Only the Pope, the Chamberlain and the Treasurer had access to the Lower Treasury.

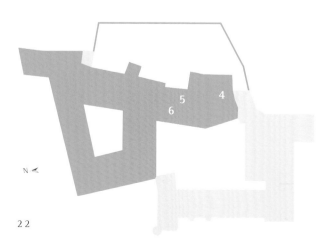

5 THE GREAT TREASURY HALL

6 THE JESUS HALL

The Great Treasury was separated into two areas by a wall. In the upper, northern, hall, a fireplace still occupies the entire width of the wall. It was here that the notaries of the Apostolic Chamber worked.

This financial service received the taxes taken from religious establishments throughout Christendom. The funds were deposited in the Treasury. The accounting ledgers were stored in the cabinets along the walls.

The Treasurer helped the Chamberlain and monitored apostolic finances, whose receipts and outgoings he recorded. They were assisted by five clerks, notaries, couriers, scribes and the personnel of the Chamber's Court of Justice, which judged many financial trials.

The Apostolic Chamber also controlled the minting of papal money, however the Mint was probably located outside the Palace.

The Jesus Hall owes its name to the monogram of Christ: I.H.S., abbreviation of the Latin "Jesus, Hominum Salvator", which decorates the walls.

This room is in the private apartments wing. It is the vestibule, because of its proximity to the main entrance of the Benedict XII's palace.

After the Popes left, as of the XVth century, the legates and vice-legates refitted this part of the Palace. This hall was converted into a dining room. In the XVIIth century, it became the hall of the Swiss Guards and the antechamber of the apartments.

Its walls were then decorated with coats of arms and the names of each vice-legate.

It was here that the cardinals attended the Pope while he dressed in the Vestry. When the master of ceremonies gave the signal, they entered the Audience Hall of the Consistory, with the Pope closing the march.

7 THE CHAMBERLAIN'S OLD CHAMBER

The Chamberlain's Old Chamber is located on the 3rd floor of the Pope's Tower.

A staircase leads to the Pope's Chamber, above.

The 14th century highly ornamental ceiling is supported by triple projecting corbels. The chamber was originally divided up into several rooms and the walls were painted with foliage scrolls on a reddish-brown background, a small area of which has been revealed on the west side. The eight masonry vaults hidden in the floor were used to keep precious objects and documents safe.

A number of mural decoration programmes between the 16th and 18th centuries obscured the original decorations. This room has been used as the Parement Chamber, a reception room and Throne room in more recent times. Military whitewash, which you can still see, covered the entire chamber throughout the 19th century.

The Chamberlain, who lived here, was the highest ranking dignitary in the Church, after the Pope. He was a sort of prime minister and was in charge of the Apostolic Chamber. As the Supreme Pontiff's right-hand man, all officers of the Court took oath before him.

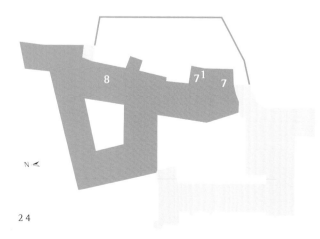

7¹ THE PAPAL VESTRY

The Papal Vestry is located on the 2nd floor of the Study Tower.

The Vestry was also used as a small library, to store papal letters from the 13th and 14th centuries.

In the 17th century, a Vice-Legate turned the old Vestry into a small chapel and the original ceiling was covered by a vault decorated with coats of arms.

This is where the Pope donned his consistorial robes: the amice, the alb and the stole. He put on red sandals, a cope adorned with a breast plate, and gloves, called chirotecae, which were trimmed with coloured brilliants. On his head he wore a camauro or small red-velvet cap, and a white mitre.

8 THE CONSISTORY HALL

The Consistory Hall occupies the ground floor of the East Wing of the cloister.

The fire that broke out in 1413 destroyed the original ceiling and decor.

On the east side, four windows were built into the wall which look out onto the gardens below. A narrower, taller bay window sheds light on the dais which stands against the Southern wall. This is where the Pope would sit, clothed in his consistorial habit. The assembly would sit on wood-panelled stone benches, which once lined the walls and have now disappeared.

The hall was used as a tribunal and audience.

The Consistory was a regular assembly during which the Pope would receive visitors and deliberate on major Church matters, be they ecclesiastic, theological, legal or political. The meetings were held either in the presence of cardinals only, i.e. the secret or ordinary consistories, or in the presence of cardinals and church or lay dignitaries, i.e. the public or extraordinary consistories. It is here that canonisations were examined and proclaimed, such as that of Saint Brigitte of Sweden.

The Consistory was also where the Pope received sovereigns, legates and ambassadors of all nations.

It was here that Clement VI greeted the famous Queen Joan of Naples, Countess of Provence and her cousin, Louis of Taranto, whom she married in 1347.

Accused of being privy to the murder of her first husband, Andrew of Hungary, she took refuge in Provence and came to plead her cause before the Holy Father.

In order to secure funds to recapture her kingdom, she sold the city of Avignon to the papacy for 80,000 florins in 1348.

Sinopia discovered during removal of the frescoes from the porch of Notre-Dame-des-Doms Cathedral. Christ Redeemer in Glory

9 SAINT JOHN'S CHAPEL

1

2

Saint John's Chapel, reserved for high dignitaries of the Church admitted to the Consistory, is on the second floor of the Chapel Tower, a small crenellated construction with a square base that flanks the East wall of the Consistory Wing. The tower houses the Saint John and Saint Martial Chapels, which were oratories devoted to more minor celebrations than those of the Great Chapel.

The Saint John Chapel has an arched vault with intersecting ribs. Light is provided by three central mullioned windows.

The themes for the decoration, executed by Matteo Giovanetti between 1346 and 1348, were taken from the lives of the two Saint Johns : on the north and east walls Saint John the Baptist, forerunner of the Messiah ; on the south and west walls Saint John the Evangelist, the first apostle and messenger of the word of Christ.

3

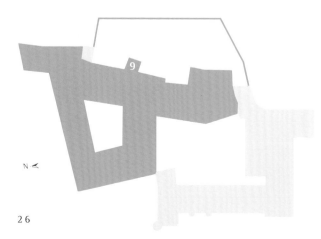

4

5

The figures are pictured mainly in landscapes and the harmony of colours and well-ordered compositions give the whole work a monumental character as well as an appearance of order and clarity. The painter takes his study in perspective a step further here by using the actual architecture of the chapel.
The holy characters' gestures are spiritual and their faces impassive even in the representation of tragic scenes, such as the beheading of Saint John and Herod's Feast, in which Salome presents Herod with Saint John's head.

1 - Saint John the Baptist, Feast of Herod
2 - Resurrection of Drusiana, at Ephesus, faces of women
3 - The vision of Patmos
4 - Saint John, the resurrection of Drusiana, detail
5 - Saint John at Ephesus, acclaimed by the Christians, carrying olive branches
6 - Recommendation of the Virgin to Saint John
7 - Saint John the Baptist

6

7

SAINT JOHN'S CHAPEL

1

2

4

3   6   7

1 - Birth of Saint John the Baptist
2 - Jesus, followed by two angels,
moving toward John the Baptist
3 - The sacrifice of Zachariah
4 - The beheading of Saint
John the Baptist
5 - South Wall of the chapel
6 - North Wall of the chapel
7 - The vocation of the son of Zebedee

5

10 THE CLOISTER

The Cloister is made up of four buildings around a courtyard. The arches which descend onto unadorned solid pillars open onto a covered passage. The upper gallery lit by gemel windows provides a passage between different buildings, which all have crenellations and machicolations. The buildings were used for different purposes. The Consistory Wing, on the East side, is the extension of the private apartments which you have just visited. It comprises two rooms built one above the other: the Consistory and the Grand Tinel or dining room.

In the South, an arched ceiling passage is built into the Guests' Wing, or Conclave Wing, and is protected by leaf doors at both ends with a room above them for operating the portcullises. The conclave wing has three storeys.

The ground floor with the upper gallery was for accommodating distinguished guests. This vast, 38-metre long room is divided by partition walls and was covered with tapestries and wall hangings. The ledgers of the Apostolic Chamber refer to this apartment as the "King's Room", then, after Charles IV of Bohemia stayed there, the "Emperor's Room". The apartment was also used during conclaves.

Above the guest apartments, near the kitchens, are the lodgings for the butlers and pantlers. These storekeepers were responsible for purchasing grain, baking bread, which was done off the premises, and for the implements needed for setting the tables. The butlers were responsible for wine supplies and for purchasing wine. The Great Storeroom, underneath the accommodation, takes up the entire ground floor and was used as a wine cellar.

On the West side, the Familiars' Wing consists of two floors above the ground floor. On the North side, the wing is flanked by the Campane Tower and on the South side by a small campanile housing the silver bell which was rung to announce meals, the opening of Court of the Rota sessions and Consistory, audiences.

Benedict XII's papal chapel occupies the North Wing. The Church of Saint Stephen was converted to house it. Built on two storeys, it is typical of Palatine chapels. The "Lower", or "dark" chapel soon stopped being used for worship and was converted into a storeroom, whilst the Upper Chapel became the "Great Chapel". A stone staircase, built onto the outside of the North gallery, was used to reach the upper level.

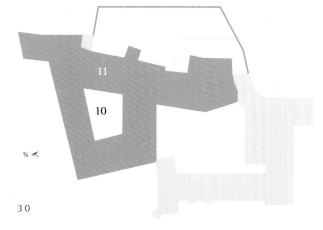

On the right, the cloister, at the end of the XVIIIth century. According to Hubert Robert. (Museum of old Avignon)

N ⊀

11 THE GRAND TINEL

At the western end of the gallery, a well built before the old Palace supplied water to the courtyard of the Cloister and the gardens located under the Consistory in the 14th c. Today the Familiars' Wing and the chapel of Benedict XII are used by the District Archives, while the south wing is occupied by the Convention Centre.

The vast hall of the Grand Tinel takes up an entire floor of the Consistory Wing. The word "tinel" was used in Italy and in the South of France for dining rooms or refectories. "Tinellum" comes from the low Latin "tina", meaning barrel or cask. It was here that banquets were held on feast days, for instance when a cardinal was appointed or a Pope crowned. On days of abstinence or on ordinary days, the Pope was served in the Petit Tinel.

This enormous hall is well lit on the East side by six windows opening out onto the gardens. Its wood-panelled, barrel-vaulted ceiling was reconstructed in the seventies and gives only a vague idea of what it was like in the 14th century. Indeed, at Clement VI's request, blue fabric studded with gold stars covered the vault to create a celestial arch. The decor was destroyed by fire in 1413, as were the frescoes of religious subjects which once adorned the walls.

Above, the Grand Tinel, before reconstruction of its panelled vault

Opposite, the Grand Tinel reconstruction of the sideboard fireplace.

The Grand Tinel,
tapestries from the Gobelins
Royal Manufacture

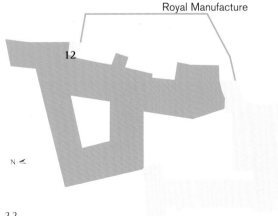

12

N

To keep the preparation work out of the sight of guests, a partition wall was built with four doors, whose supports can still be seen in the walls, near where the fireplace is located. This area, known as the "Dressoir" or food dressing area, communicates with the kitchen. Here the food was put onto plates and kept warm in front of the fireplace before it was served. The chief steward, the butler, the pantler, the water steward, and a number of other servants waited here in case they were needed, as did the master carver who cut up the food.

During the conclave, the arches separating the Grand Tinel from the Guests' Apartments and from the Parement Chamber were hollowed out to give more room to the Cardinals.

Once the conclave was over, the arches were filled in again, the painted decoration restored and the doors and windows opened up. The rooms then returned to normal.

Banquets followed a strict protocol which governed where guests were seated and the type of dishes they were served, in keeping with the dictates of alternate shrove and abstinence days. The post of chief steward was held by an officer who seated guests close to or far away from the Pope, depending on their importance.

The papal table stood on a dais, along the wall opposite the "Dressoir". The Pope ate there alone, seated on a Cathedra, or throne, under a sumptuous canopy.

Guests sat on wooden benches that lined the walls, the cardinals to the East, other guests to the West. Trestle tables were arranged in a U shape and food was served from the centre of the room.

12 THE UPPER KITCHEN

Under Benedict XII, the kitchen was situated on the north side of the Consistory, and communicated with the Grand Tinel by an open staircase near the main fireplace in the "Dressoir".

During Clement VI's pontificate, a new Kitchen Tower was built. One of the floors was called the "larder"; another the "grape room", which is where fruit was preserved. The top floor of the tower was the Upper Kitchen, which was lit by three windows separated by a depressed arch. The walls form a square at the base. Above, four squinches are used to take the square into an octagonal shape, creating an 18-metre tower. The central hearth, at ground level, is enclosed by a low wall, where roasting cooks piled grills and spits above each other, so that large quantities of food could be cooked at the same time. The abundance of spit-roasted and grilled meats was typical of medieval cooking in grand households.

On the north side of the Kitchen Tower, stand the Latrines Tower, or Ice Tower, and the Trouillas Tower.

Below,
fireplace hood

The list of victuals bought for Pope Clement VI's coronation still exists. The event took place outside the palace and required 118 oxen, 1,023 sheep, 101 calves, 914 kids, 60 pigs, 69 hundredweight of bacon, 1,500 capons, 3,043 fowl, 7,428 chickens, 1,195 geese, 50,000 tarts, 6 hundredweight of almonds, 2 hundredweight of sugar, 39,980 eggs and 95,000 loaves of bread.

13 SAINT MARTIAL'S CHAPEL

1

2

3

4

Originally called the Tinel Chapel, Saint Martial's Chapel occupied the third floor of the Chapel Tower, built in 1338 during Benedict XII's pontificate. It was built over the Consistory's Saint John's Chapel. It was devoted to Saint Martial during Clement VI's reign.

Clement VI, born into a family of minor Limousin nobles, attached great importance to Saint Martial, who evangelised the Limousin in the 3rd century. Local legend made him into an apostle, said to have been sent to Gaul by Saint Peter, which would accredit him with being the forerunner of the Avignon Popes. The choice of an iconographic programme devoted to Saint Martial was proof of Clement VI's determination to strengthen the legitimacy of having a pontifical residence far from Rome. The pope asked Matteo Giovanetti to decorate the walls of the chapel with scenes from the saint's life. The painter carried out the work with other artists between 1344 and 1346.

During the conclaves, the cardinals deliberated and voted in the chapel, where the holy sacraments were displayed permanently on the altar.

This chapel has had a troubled history (fire, conversion into a foundry under the military, vandalism...) and must be restored.

5

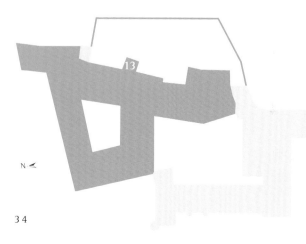

6   7   8

1 - Saint Martial, resurrection of Austriclinian
2 - Funeral of Martial, faces
3 - Soldiers
4 - Crucifixion, eastern wall
5 - Saint Martial receiving his
miraculous staff from Saint Peter
6 - Group of men
7 - Soldiers of the Duke Stephen, camp
8 - Vision of the martyrdom of Saint Paul
9 - Vault

Above a painted faux-marble crepidoma, or base, there are 35 episodes told in 42 paintings, which start at the northern vault and spiral round to the west wall. Letters of the alphabet are used to put the paintings in sequence.

The artist incorporates the chapel's architecture in his work : the vault's complex decoration was divided into eight compartments around the four intersecting ribs. A starry blue night sky pervades the composition and boldly forms a cross that intersects the ribs.

The somewhat urban setting shows trompe-l'oeil buildings, with little landscape. The characters are set in colourful architecture - fortresses, churches and loggias - seen from different angles. These extremely lively scenes are heightened by piquant details and individualised portraits. The treatment is less contemplative, less remote than in Saint John's Chapel and alternates between narrative realism and the miraculous.

Matteo Giovanetti balances out this lavish account by a unity of colour containing lapis-lazuli blue, grey and brown decorated with gold, which reveals here his liking for imaginary architecture and complex perspectives.

9

1 - Christ
followed by a procession of saints
2 - North Wall, angels singing

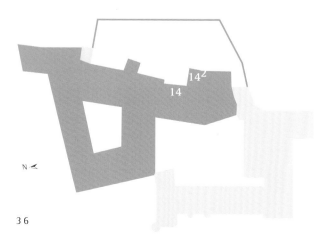

14 THE PAREMENT CHAMBER
14² THE STUDY

The Parement Chamber is located in the eastern wing of the private apartments above the Jesus Hall. It is the antechamber to the Pope's chamber, which are on the North side.

The term "parement" describes for all the tapestries that decorated the walls and seating. Later on, the Parement Chamber was called the "Parade Chamber".

The room was originally covered by a wood-panelled, barrel-vaulted ceiling, similar to the one in the Grand Tinel, which was also destroyed by fire in 1413. There was a fireplace, an altar, two seats and two wrought-iron candelabras. The Pope sat on a dais underneath a canopy. On the eastern wall, vestiges of the trompe-l'oeil decoration give insight into how the room's rich murals must have looked like.

The Parement Chamber underwent extensive alterations over the centuries as the marks on the walls show.

The two levels of arcading on the north and south wall correspond to the floors put in by the military to increase the palace's habitable space. Similar traces appear in many rooms of the palace.

The Pope and the cardinals held secret consistories here. Important figures were also given audiences here.

This is where the Pope presented the Golden Rose to the person he wished to honour - usually a sovereign - on the 4th Sunday of Lent.

The National Museum of the Middle Ages in Paris has a Golden Rose in fine gold, weighing 305 grams, which dates from the early days of the Avignon papacy. It comprises a rose branch with a flower in bloom decorated with a sapphire at the centre.

The Study Tower, given over to the Pope's personal work and financial inspectorate, was built in 1337. Two of its walls are in fact the walls of the Pope's Tower and of the Parement Chamber. Its rectangular ground plan is uneven. There is, from bottom to top : at garden level, a cellar ; then the Treasury's secret chamber; above this, the Papal Vestry ; and lastly Benedict XII's study. In 1365, in the orchard below the Study Tower, Pope Urban V built a pleasure gallery called La Roma, which was decorated by Matteo Giovanetti. It was destroyed in the 19th century, when the Palace was turned into barracks.

The Study is set slightly below the Pope's chamber, to which it is connected by a narrow corridor. The room had a wooden ceiling and its walls were adorned with painted decoration of red flowers on a blue background that has not been restored to date.

The Study floor was uncovered in 1963. This tiled floor comprises strips of monochromatic green and brown glazed tiles, which alternate with strips of figurative tiles, arranged diagonally. The decorative themes are varied. There are plant and animal motifs, birds and many fish ; geometric designs - chequered patterns, rosettes, interlacing spirals and heraldic motifs as well. Only one tile has a human figure on it. The Study is the only room in the Palace that sill has its original 14th century floor, the tiled floors in the other rooms are reproductions from 1969.

15 THE POPE'S CHAMBER

2

1

The Pope's Chamber is situated in the heart of the Angel Tower, between the Chamberlain's Chamber and the Upper Treasury, and contain part of the treasure and a library.

This room is divided up by moving partition walls. The Pope usually slept here with the attendants called cubiculars who served him. He sometimes gave private audiences here, too.

The room is ventilated by a tall opening near the corner fireplace, and gets its light from two windows covered simply with wax-coated fabric stretched on wooden frames and, in some cases, embellished with painted decorative motifs. The account ledgers mention several payments made to glass painters, but refer only to the chapels and rooms in which ceremonies were held. The stained glass windows that you see here are reproductions.

The furniture is 14th and 16th century, but is not from the Palace. In Clement VII's time, the room contained a bed with crushed velvet and emerald taffeta curtains, a chair, a table, a stool and a number of chests lining the walls containing linen for the Pope's use. As all the Popes were very fond of birds, they sometimes kept caged nightingales in their rooms.

N ≺

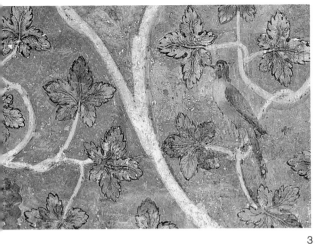

3   4

Beneath the ceiling, of which only four beams are original, runs a quatrefoil frieze with illegible motifs. Against a blue background, abundant vine and oak leaves intertwine, populated with birds and squirrels. Like the painted draperies of the crepidomas, these tempera paintings were extensively restored in 1934. In the window recesses, fine decoration sets off the Gothic arcading in trompe-l'oeil, which appears to bear bird cages - some with, some without occupants - treated in perspective.

These decorations may have been executed between 1336 and 1337. However, a good deal of controversy surrounds the dates and the artists who worked on them. It may be assumed that some were carried out by a French studio, under Jean d'Albon. The abstract pictorial space and the lack of perspective are well and truly in the French tradition. However, the upper register of the walls and especially the motifs on the window recesses, which were not done schematically, but in perspective, that is they appear to be in actual space, are in the Italian tradition.

Details of murals:
1 - Scrolls of vine leaves and bird (detail)
2 - Squirrel on scrolls of oak leaves
3 - Scrolls of grape leaves and bird
4 - Decor of cages

5 - Corner fireplace

5

1

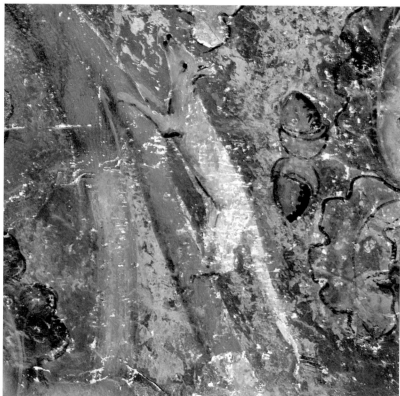

2

Details of murals:

1 - Bird set on scrolls of grape leaves

2 - Weasel on scrolls of oak leaves

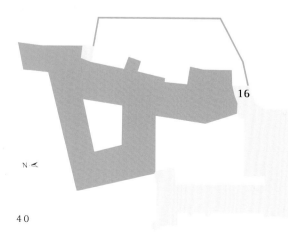

16

N

16 THE STAG ROOM

1

2

3

The Stag Room, which marks the passage from the old to the new palace, is situated on the 4th of the Wardrobe Tower's five storeys.

On the ground floor, are the "ovens", in fact the room where the pope bathed. The two following stories correspond to the wardrobes. Above the Stag Room is the Pope's personal chapel, dedicated to St. Michael.

The Stag Room was Pope Clement VI's study. The Pope had a bed and his own personal library set up here ; the room also contained two chests lined with watered silk. The Pontiff's lavish tastes doubtless explain the room's rather original decor.

The room derived its name from a frescoes of staghunting, most of which disappeared when the room was remodelled during the 18th century.

1 - Episode from a stag hunt
2 - 3 - Bird ferreters in the bushes
4 - Scenes of fishing around a pond

4

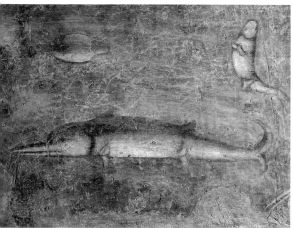

1

2

The 14th century ceiling is richly decorated.
The secular subjects of the frescoes depict the seigniorial pleasures of the day, hunting and fishing.
Buried under several coats of military paint, the frescoes of the Stag Room were miraculously preserved.
As in the Pope's chamber, the tiles are a reconstruction effected on the basis of the floor discovered in the Studium of the Study Tower.

1 - 2 - Fish and ducks
3 - Gathering fruit
4 - Under the frame, two friezes :
on the upper level, hunting scenes,
below, a frieze of shields
5 - Scene of a return from falcon hunting
6 - A bird ferreter in
the branches of a tree

Beneath a narrow strip of sky, an entire forest is painted on the walls; tall trees of various species, bushes laden with fruit and flowers, and a parterre of tall-growing herbaceous plants and flowers. In this luxuriant natural setting, birds and animals are prey to hawkers, catching them with bird calls or decoys. A hunter lets his ferret loose on a rabbit, which looks round and takes flight.
Four people, fishing by different means, gather around a pool in which pike and other freshwater fish are swimming.
A number of painters worked on these frescoes. This is seen in for the changes in style in which some of the characters are depicted, for example, between those ferreting and the children.
The panoramic scene is painted in perspective. In the pool scene, a third dimension is suggested in the contours of most of the faces, which are, without a doubt, the work of Italian artists. Perhaps they were supervised by Matteo Giovanetti ?
Secular subjects of this type were used in French and Italian tapestries from the 13th century on, but were dealt with in a more conventional manner, placing the emphasis on decorative effect.
In the Stag Room, the bucolic theme is interpreted in a more naturalistic and descriptive fashion.
Here, Italian artistic concepts serve the French courtly ideal.

3

4

5

6

The North Sacristy is in the South Wing, which runs from east to west and forms an angle with the previous building. Its layout is asymmetrical and it has two vaulted bays with intersecting ribs. This type of architecture, and the introduction of carved decoration, mark the difference between this and Benedict XII's palace, in which there are a greater number of wood-panelled vaults and ceilings.

The bridge that Innocent VI had built in 1360 to link his private apartments to the Great Chapel terminated in the first bay. It has since disappeared, however the access can still be seen near the window.

It was in the Sacristy that the Supreme Pontiff changed his vestments during ceremonies held in the Great Chapel.

Most of the plaster mouldings on show here were gifts from European cities. They portray political and religious figures or prestigious guests whom the Popes received at the Palace.

The Great Chapel, which is devoted to the two apostles, Peter and Paul, was built by Clement VI. Despite the spread of the Black Death in 1348, it took less than 4 years to complete it.

The single nave is 52 metres long, 15 metres wide and 20 metres tall. It is covered by seven vaulted bays with pointed arches, whose ribs descend onto slim columns. It is lit by four central mullioned bay windows in the south, and by two double mullioned windows on each of the gabled walls. Before the installation of the stained glass windows, ordered from a master glassmaker in Avignon, the windows were covered with orlcloth stretched on wooden frames, which Matteo Giovanetti embellished with red, yellow and green arabesques. The legates had the coats of arms of the reigning Popes, which can be seen on the east and west walls, painted during the 16th and 17th centuries.

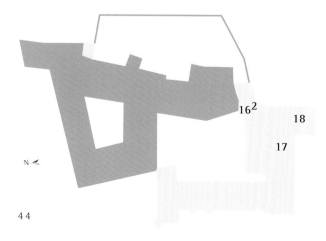

16²

18

17

N ◄

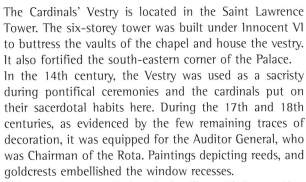

The Cardinals' Vestry is located in the Saint Lawrence Tower. The six-storey tower was built under Innocent VI to buttress the vaults of the chapel and house the vestry. It also fortified the south-eastern corner of the Palace.

In the 14th century, the Vestry was used as a sacristy during pontifical ceremonies and the cardinals put on their sacerdotal habits here. During the 17th and 18th centuries, as evidenced by the few remaining traces of decoration, it was equipped for the Auditor General, who was Chairman of the Rota. Paintings depicting reeds, and goldcrests embellished the window recesses.

This room has a vaulted, arched ceiling with intersecting ribs, which descend onto clusters of small columns. One of the keystones bears Innocent VI's coat of arms.

The casts are copies of the funeral effigies of Popes Clement V, Clement VI, Innocent VI and Urban V, as no Pontiff was ever buried in the palace.

The first three bays make up the choir; the altar is situated in the first bay, and the Pope's Cathedra stood under a golden canopy in the second. Green hangings decorated with red roses were hung on the walls; rugs and mats covered the floors.

The cardinals and twelve cantors occupied the third bay. They were separated from the faithful by a barrier called a Chancel.

From Clement VI's reign on, the Great Chapel was the scene of pontifical ceremonies, every aspect of which was governed by the Ordos, or guides to Roman ceremonial. Fifty-eight liturgical festivals were held there: Sunday masses, canonisation masses, the mass for the last Sunday of Lent and the mass before the Golden Rose was presented to a Christian prince.

Of all the sumptuous ceremonies, the papal coronation was the scene of exceptional pomp and magnificence.

19 THE CHAMBERLAIN'S CHAMBER

20 THE NOTARIES' CHAMBER

The Chamberlain's New Chamber is in the Great Dignitaries Wing. This building has a rectangular ground plan, the western façade of which runs along the present Palace Square and houses new areas on one or two floors. This was made necessary by the pontifical administration's expansion during Clement VI's reign.

On the first floor, you will find the Chamberlain's new apartments, those of the treasury, notaries, the Treasurer's chamber and the portcullis room, which defended the Champeaux Gate. The conclave gallery which served the cubiculum or sleeping chamber is on the next floor. The Watch Tower rises above the Chamberlain's chamber.

In the 14th century, this chamber was divided into three by partitions and there was a fireplace with a mantel. As you can see, there has been an attempt to reconstruct it in stucco.

This is the workroom of the notaries of the Apostolic Chamber. They were responsible for expediting current financial affairs, preparing contracts and letters of the chamberlain, and verifying the accounts of the tax collectors.

In the mid - 18th century, the walls of this room were decorated at mid-height with a frieze in the Pompeian style, consisting of mythological scenes painted in cartouches alternating with cupids, supposedly ordered by vice-legate Pascal Aquaviva d'Aragona.

A north-west gate leads to the watchman's rounds ; another, to the north-east, opens on a staircase installed inside the wall leading to the Conclave gallery in the Portcullis chamber, below, and to the Great Promenade, on the upper level.

This traffic network is typical of the New Palace ; it enabled the defence of the entire Grand Dignitaries Wing.

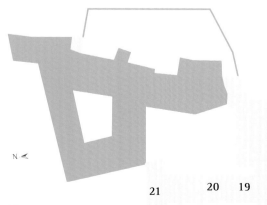

N ◄

21   20   19

21 THE GREAT DIGNITARIES' TERRACES

The terraces originally surmounted part of the New Palace
buildings, the Great Promenade Gallery, and the Great
Dignitaries' wing, where you are now standing.
As a chronicler of the day remarked : "although in this
part of the palace all the edifices are majestic and
admirable in aspect, three areas, however, surpass all the
others : the Audience Hall, the Great Chapel and the
upper terraces. All three are so remarkably structured that
no palace in the world has anything to equal them."
The terrace affords a magnificent view of Avignon and
the region, Villeneuve-les-Avignon and the Rhone.

Large sculptures decorated the lateral niches. Only one now remains, under the central canopy, which has been identified as Saint Peter, to whom the Chapel is devoted. The lintel over the double door represents the Last Judgement. As a result of the damage it has sustained, particularly during the 19th century, all that remains is the representation of the damned being thrown into the flames of Hell. The bases of the uprights are in better condition and are reminiscent of those in Saint John's Cathedral in Lyon.

This landing, or loggia, forms the court in front of the Great Chapel. It gets its light from the Palace square - which is now the Courtyard of Honour - through the Indulgence Window.

This is where the Holy Father gave his triple blessing to the crowd gathered in the Courtyard of Honour and where the tiara was placed on the Pope's head during the coronation ceremony.

The Great Chapel Door is the most important group of sculpture in the palace. The archivolt is comprised of two arches. The taller of the two contains 12 figures, the shorter only 10. All the heads were broken off during the French Revolution.

In the 19th century, military engineers bored a door into the tympanum and altered a staircase to gain access to the dormitories which had been set up in the Great Chapel. This operation completely destroyed the left-hand side of the lintel and the tympanum, as well as part of the archivolt.

N ◄

23

22

23 THE GREAT STAIRCASE OF HONOUR

In 1346, construction began on the Great Staircase of Honour that serves the Great Chapel. Jean de Louvres had to double the thickness of the Audience Hall wall to house the bays and intersecting ribs as they increased in height. The structure, formed from two straight flights of stairs that turn back toward the core wall, was an innovation found only in Italy at the time.

The wide staircase is lit by windows giving out onto the courtyard, and is flanked by rooms used as guard posts. In days gone by at each pillar there were three wooden doors with heavy iron-clad leaves, which were used to protect the staircase.

The magnitude which Jean de Louvres gave it was uncommon for the time and leant itself perfectly to the solemn majesty of the grand pontifical ceremonies of the day.

As you go down the staircase, you will notice an inscription in a cartouche, which refers to how the staircase was rebuilt by Vice-Legate Lascaris in 1659, before Louis XIV's visit.

24 LA GRANDE AUDIENCE

The Great Audience Hall has the second largest nave in the southern wing. It has the same dimensions as the Great Chapel, which is directly above it, but is not as high.

The different levels of ground beneath the Great Audience Hall provided space for a lower hall to house the Theology School.

The Great Audience Hall is Jean de Louvres's masterpiece. Its proportions are indeed remarkable: 52 metres long by 16.80 metres wide and 11 metres high. It is divided into two naves by five pillars, on which the intersecting ribs of the vaults rest. On the wall side, the ribs rest on sculpted imposts with representations of mythical beasts.

The Great Audience Hall housed the Court of Apostolic Causes, the standing judicial body against whose judgements no appeal was possible, which was organised in an auditors' college. From 1336, it was called the Court of the Rota, from the Latin "Rota" meaning "wheel", on account of the round bench on which the judges sat. A barrier separated them from the rest of the hall. An inscription on the north wall indicates where Bernard Hugues de Cardalhac sat. He was an auditor from 1316 to 1355.

Another decoration, also destroyed in the 19th century, depicted a Calvary. The painting, whose beautiful remains are still visible, was set above the altar, which stood a against the east wall.

The court assigned ecclesiastic benefices throughout Christendom, heard hundreds of appeals, and corresponded throughout Europe. It could deal with up to 8,000 letters and 10,000 petitions a year. The court sat in the eastern bay where the keystones bear the coats of arms of Clement VI and those of Rome, S.P.Q.R., which stand for "The Senate and the People of Rome". This motto is a reminder of the Pontiff and the pontifical administration's Roman origins. An enormous Last Judgement, which no longer exists, once adorned the northern wall. This iconographic theme is directly related to the place's function and underscores the court's infallibility.

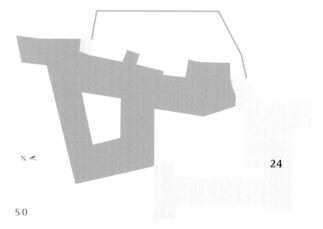

N

24

THE PROPHETS' FRESCO

The shape of the vault has determined the arrangement of figures on a starry azure background. They are divided up into groups of four rows. Kings David and Solomon accompany the four most important prophets. All are named and bear a banderole with a long quotation. The painter gave each of the prophets a powerful individuality. Despite the subject's severity, the painter suggests space and breathes life into the characters and to the gestures, which either balance or contrast with one another, due to the positioning of the figures - profile, full face or three-quarters.

THE IMPOSTS

The sculptures that adorn the imposts onto which the vaults descend contribute to the decorative quality. They represent a wide variety of mythical beasts: a quadruped with a monkey's head, a winged dragon crouching, the bust of a crowned man strangling two geese, and a boar armed with a sword. There are still a few traces of the red and yellow ochre that originally covered the bases.

25 THE THEOLOGY ROOM   THE CHAPEL OF BENEDICT

Located to the east of the Clement VI's new Palace, the main access is on the place de la Mirande.

Embedded in the rock under the Great Audience Hall, the room is illuminated by two windows cut in the eastern wall. The ribs of its vault, consisting of four casements, rest on a central pillar without a capital. Two doors with removable staircases provided access to the interior of the Palace.

It is in this room that the magister palatii taught theology and gave courses open to the public.

Since the prison was moved in 1871, the Archives have occupied the north wing of the Palace of Benedict XII, and part of the Familiars' wing, the Campane tower and the Trouillas tower.

The papal chapel of Benedict XII was still roofless in the 19th century when the architect Revoil undertook his restoration to install the District Archives in 1883.

With its four kilometres of shelving, it groups an impressive amount of archives. Other documents are stored in the lower parts of the Campane tower.

The Reading Room occupies the upper west gallery of the cloister and forms an angle with the Curator's offices, on the north side.

Access to the archives is through the place du Palais, to the left of the entrance of the Convention Centre.

District Archives
Campane tower

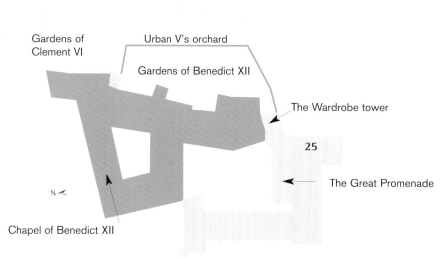

Gardens of Clement VI

Urban V's orchard

Gardens of Benedict XII

The Wardrobe tower

25

N

Chapel of Benedict XII

The Great Promenade

AREAS NOT OPEN TO THE PUBLIC

Above, the bath-house

THE PAPAL GARDENS

The Popes' Palace gardens are on two levels : Benedict XII's garden and Urban V's orchard. As was commonplace during the Middle Ages, the gardens are enclosed by ramparts.

Clement VI had a large fountain called a "griffon" built in the southern part of Benedict XII's garden. On top of the inner wall of the ramparts, a tank was installed to supply water to the fountain. To fill the tank a machine - probably a noria or bucket water-wheel - was added in 1334 above the garden well. This was also used to irrigate the grounds and to supply water to the steamrooms, or baths, on the first floor of the Wardrobe Tower.

The gardens contained potted plants, rose bushes and banks of violets, fruit trees, vines on trellises or arbours planted along the walls, and a large vegetable garden with a variety of vegetables : white and green cabbage, spinach, chard, parsley and leeks, to name but a few. Aromatic and medicinal plants, such as marjoram, sage, fennel and borage, were also cultivated.

The Popes of Avignon, like the great sovereigns of the time, owned different species of wild animals, which they bought or were given as gifts by the great princes of Europe or faraway lands. John XXII built up a sizeable collection of animals, which included a bear, a lion, a camel, boar, deer and wild cats. His successors kept the menagerie and expanded it. The deer keeper, or "wild animal keeper" was responsible for looking after them.

THE GREAT PROMENADE

This long gallery, 36-metres long, built originally with seven vaulted bays on intersecting ribs, was used for promenades. The proximity of the papal apartments made access easy. The pontiff and the cardinals met there. Dinners were also served there.

The Wardrobe tower

It was during the construction of the Wardrobe tower that the name of Jean de Louvres, architect to Pope Clement VI, appeared in the account books. The new pope, no doubt who considered his predecessor's apartments too small, had the tower built during the first year of his pontificate. It has five levels.

On the ground floor, are the "ovens", in fact the room where the pope bathed.

The two following floors correspond to the wardrobes. The upper wardrobe includes the pope's personal linen and ornaments in closets and chests. Chamberlains slept there, responsible for guarding these riches. The lower wardrobe was used mostly as a furniture storehouse and became necessary because of the amount of furniture acquired under Clement VI. The functions of these two floors gave the tower its name. Above the Stag Room is the pope's personal chapel, dedicated to St. Michael. Matteo Giovanetti decorated it with a fresco representing the "history of the angels of all provinces". This theme then wrongly gave its name to the Pope's tower or Angel's tower nearby. Of these frescoes, only the sinopias remain today.

1

2

The Convention Centre

Created in 1976, the Convention Centre occupies all of the Conclave and a part of the Familiars' Wing, in the palace of Benedict XII. It encompasses a fraction of the Grand Dignitaries' Wing in the palace of Clement VI.

In the palace of Benedict XII

The Conclave wing (1337 and 1338) forms the south wing of the palace of Benedict XII and has three levels. In the lower part, partially embedded in the rock and opening onto the south gallery of the cloister, the great cellar was used as a wine store. Today, it has been converted into a projection and conference room, built on an inclined plane. Above the cellar, in the large hall formed by the bottlemaking and basketmaking shops, a modulable multipurpose room has been installed. The Guests' apartment, or Conclave room, occupies the third level. Important guests were lodged here and cardinals gathered here for conclaves during the election of the pope. Depending on circumstances, partitions and curtains divided this large area. The walls were decorated with delicate paintings as shown by the fragments found on the north and east walls. The installation of the Convention Centre permitted the restoration of the vault. With its facing bleacher seats, it is a council-type chamber making up the plenary assembly hall. In addition to the Conclave wing, the facilities of the Convention Centre also occupy the Cardinal Blanc tower and part of the Familiars' wing in the palace of Benedict XII.

3

1 - Conclave Hall : capacity 560

2 - The Treasurer's Chamber : capacity 170

3 - The Great Cellar : capacity 237

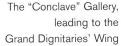

The "Conclave" Gallery,
leading to the
Grand Dignitaries' Wing

Above,
The Angle Tower,
basket-handle arch window

In the palace of Clement VI

The Grand Dignitaries' wing, built between 1345 and 1347, forms the western side of the palace of Clement VI. The Champeaux gate marks its middle. The spacious North Guards Room has beautiful vaults with intersecting ribs and interesting sculpted rib imposts. It is now the reception area of the Convention Centre. Installed as a projection/conference room, the Treasurer's Chamber is just above the North Guards Room with which it communicates by a staircase. Another entrance leads to the Conclave gallery, one of the architectural marvels of the palace. Projecting into the Courtyard of Honour, this elegant corridor connects the Conclave wing to the Great Promenade. Its vault, formed by a small series of intersecting ribs is the only example of gothic lanceolate style in the palace and the sculptures of the rib imposts are remarkably fine.

Next to the Conclave Gallery, the "cubiculars'"chamber takes its name from Bernard de Saint Etienne, cubicular to the pope in 1370. The lovely wooden frame is highlighted by a large bay opening between the two turrets of the façade. Today it is used as a commission room. Just above the cubiculars' chamber, the Herses chamber controls the access to the Champeaux gate. Its sculpted rib imposts are remarkable. The last wing contains small rooms and resting rooms. The Angel tower, built in 1346, was used to monitor the two gates (Notre Dame to the north and Champeaux to the west) ; it also included the Treasurer's apartments. Notre Dame gate (1348), connecting the Angle tower to Cardinal Blanc's tower, is topped by the Notre Dame portcullis room and the so-called Four Windows chamber, the restoration of which revealed a splendid Renaissance door.

1

During the legates' period

During the 15th century, when the Pope took up residence in Rome again, the administration of Avignon and the Comtat Venaissin was entrusted to a legate who represented the Pope. The first legate's job was to complete the restoration work that the palace required, which had suffered extensive damage during the two sieges endured by the last Avignon Pope, Benedict XIII. Another programme of works, began after a terrible fire that had spread from the kitchen to the whole of the East Wing in 1413.

The most famous legate of all was undoubtedly Giuliano Della Rovere, the future Pope Julius II, who was to be the benefactor to Raphael and Michelangelo and who commissioned the Sistine Chapel. Under his legateship, the Bishopric of Avignon became an Archbishopric. He ordered extensive alteration and restoration work to the palace, but never lived there. He lived in the Archbishop's residence, which he had magnificently decorated. This building, now the Petit Palais Museum, has been remarkably well restored and today houses a collection of Italian and Provençal primitives.

During the 16th century, the legates occupied only part of the palace. Among them, Francois de Clermont-Lodève built a reception hall, La Mirande, in Urban V's orchard, and Georges d'Armagnac embellished the decoration in the Great Chapel with stained glass and paintings of coats-of-arms.

In the 17th century, the Pope was only represented in Avignon by Vice-Legates, all of whom were Italian. The legates in office would always be one of the Pope's nephews, who also fulfilled the function of secretary of state. The Pope remained in Rome and left it to his lieutenant's good offices to govern Avignon and the Comtat Venaissin. The administration was in the

2

3

hands of the Italian clergy, and this sparked off serious popular rebellions in the mid-17th century. The Vice-Legates occupied only the Popes' former private apartments - the northern part of the palace had already fallen into disuse.

4   5

The legates' apartments

At the end of the 18th century, the legates lived in the buildings east of the Courtyard of Honour. The Jesus hall then became the Swiss hall. In the Chamberlain's hall, called the Light Horses' hall or Cavaliers' hall, the vice-legate installed his throne. The old papal vestry was converted into a chapel. The summer and winter apartments occupied the western section of the private apartments, gone today. The noble apartments, built in the orchard, overlooked the rampart of Benedict XII. The old Herses room at the Peyrolerie gate was used as a bedroom for the vice-legate and the Small Audience room became the Hall of Arms. In the 18th century the Great Chapel was no longer used. The Old Consistory, called the "burned room" was turned into a court for playing the popular jeu de paume game during the 16th century. The Familiars' wing and the Campane tower contained the papal prisons. The Swiss guards had their quarters in the upper galleries of the cloister called the "Swiss courtyard". The chapel of Benedict XII contained the archives of the canons of Notre-Dame-des-Doms.

The revolution

The last of the vice-legates, Philippe Gasoni, was forced to flee Avignon under pressure of anti-papist revolutionaries on 12 June 1790. The palace was converted into a prison for the enemies of the revolution. Commandant Jourdan, known as "the headcutter" had just moved in when Avignon and the Comtat Venaissin were proclaimed French territory on 14 September, 1791. During this troubled period, among the most memorable events were the so-called "Glacier" massacres which took place in that tower (also called the Latrine tower) on the night of 16 to 17 October, 1791. About sixty "suspects" some still alive, were thrown into the Latrine ditch as reprisal for the murder of the patriot Lescuyer. During the terror, the jails of the palace overflowed with prisoners. Finally, despite the decision reached by the Convention (18 January, 1793), the palace escaped destruction, but was subjected to damage and plunder.

The military occupation

At the beginning of the 19th century, the palace was assigned to the Army. It was only in 1821 that it was converted into a barracks. In trying to restore the premises, the military caused irreparable damage. During this period, most of the palace rooms were divided in two by floors built across them. The prison, property of the district since 1811, occupied a large section of the palace of Benedict XII until 1871. The military destroyed la Roma in 1837, then Benedict XII's rampart. In 1848, the ruined fort of the Trouillas tower was demolished for safety reasons. In 1857, the ravelin, built by Lomellini in front of the Champeaux gate, suffered the same fate. At the time, most of the rooms of the palace were cut in half by floors; the traces of these installations remain today.

The frescoes, in particular from the chapels, were ravaged and the details removed to be sold. The evacuation of the Army only took place in 1906, when the restoration work decided by the Historical monuments authority began.

1 - View of the palace with a vice-legate's cortege oil painting by Claude Marie Gordot, 1774 (Calvet museum, Avignon)
2 - Costume of the Swiss guards (Museum of old Avignon)
3 - Coat of arms of a vice-legate
4 - Massacres of the "Glacier", October 1791 (District archives)
5 - Small audience hall used by military engineers ca. 1900 (City archives, Bartesago collection)

THE PALACE AFTER THE DEPARTURE OF THE POPES

1

2

THE RESTORATION

1 - Conclave Wing before the
restoration
2 - After restoration in 1976
(RMG archives)
3 - The Conclave Wing,
during restoration,
and the creation of the Convention
Centre, between 1970 and 1976.
(RMG archives)

In 1860, Viollet-le-Duc drafted a restoration plan which the Franco-Prussian War fortunately prevented. This plan recommended the destruction of the vaults of the Grand Audience hall so that it would form one great nave with the Great Chapel. After the transfer of the prison to the rue Banasterie in 1871 the district archives were installed in the buildings and in the refurbished chapel of Benedict XII. In 1907, work began, conducted by Henri Nodet, architect of the Historical Monuments authority. The floors left by the Army were destroyed in the Grand Audience hall and the Great Chapel. Then the Small Audience hall (1912-1913) and the Grand dignitaries wing (1921-1922) were restored. By 1926, the palace of Clement VI was practically restored. Work on the Old Palace then started by the refurbishing of the Grand Tinel then the Upper Kitchen. In 1933, the two turrets of the Champeaux Gate were rebuilt. The restoration of the Pope's Chambers lasted from 1934 to 1937. The war interrupted the

3

works which resumed in 1946 with the Consistory and the Angel tower. Then restoration was begun on the east wing and the private apartements, which were in a total state of ruin. The Parement Chamber, the Theology room (1967) and the Jesus room, completed in 1968, were all restored. In the Conclave wing, heavily damaged by the Army, the construction of the Convention Centre began in 1970 and lasted until 1976. Several restoration "campaigns" for the frescoes were carried out between 1960 and 1973. Between 1978 and 1987 the Grand Tinel was fitted with its "ship's hull" vaulted ceiling ; the Great Treasury and the Lower Treasury were restored. Restoration of all the arches along the western gallery of the Benedict XII cloister has only recently been completed. The north terrace of the Grand dignitaries wing is now open to the public, offering an outstanding panorama of the surrounding landscape. In 1997, the restoration program turned to refurbishing the St. Lawrence tower. At the same time, a scientific study mission of the frescoes of the Saint Martial chapel was conducted so as to establish a diagnosis before the restoration operations begin on the paintings by Matteo Giovanetti.

1

2

THE PALACE, AN EXCEPTIONAL PATRIMONIAL AND CULTURAL SITE

The papal palace is considered to be one of the most widely visited monuments in France with more than 500,000 visitors per year. The areas visited represent about one third of the entire palace. The Convention Centre occupies all the Conclave Wing and the upper floor of the Grand Dignitaries wing. During the summer, the Honour Courtyard is used by the Avignon Theatre Festival. Also during the summer, the Great Chapel is used for retrospective exhibits of works by great artists and sculptors (Botero, Dubuffet, Picasso, Rodin) or historic exhibits (History of Weaving, Treasures of Clockmaking).

1 - the Honour Courtyard during the Avignon Theatre Festival (RMG archives)
2 - the Great Chapel, Rodin exhibit, 1996
2 - the Great Chapel, History of Weaving exhibit 1997 (RMG archives)

3

THE DOMS ROCK

The highest point of Avignon, the Doms Rock garden offers an outstanding view of the palace, the city and its surroundings. From the terraces, the nearby hills called the "dentelles de Montmirail", Mount Ventoux, the Luberon hills and the Alpilles can all be seen. At the foot of the rock, the truncated Benezet bridge tries to cross the Rhone towards Villeneuve-les-Avignon.

A remarkable observation and defensive site, we know that the oppidum was peopled as of the Neolithic Age. In the 15th century, windmills were built on top of this high rock. In 1650, the castle, at the time used to store gunpowder, exploded and the rock, uninhabited from then on, became a popular promenade area. The access ramps connecting it to the palace were built in the second half of the 18th century. During the Revolution, a cemetery was installed. It was only in 1830 that work began on the public gardens, with plantings and terraces. From the garden, you may take a staircase to the Benezet bridge then to the façade of the rampart, west of the rock. This itinerary passes by the Dog's Tower (15th century) - so named because it was used as a pound - to reach the fortified castle. You may also reach the garden from the Rhone by taking the north staircase (173 steps) ; by the Mill slope from the Palace Square ; and in the east by Saint Anne's staircase which extends the Pope's Promenade (by the rue de la Peyrolerie and the orchard of Urban V).

Map of Avignon,
the Palace Square
and the rock of Doms

NOTRE-DAME-DES-DOMS

North of the palace, the present cathedral is a magnificent example of Roman influence on the Romanesque Provençal style. It was built in the 12th century on the site of a paleo-Christian basilica and an earlier edifice, consecrated in 1069.

Modified many times over the centuries, the bishop's church was less imposing originally than it is today. The Roman influence is seen everywhere . The porch, added at the end of the 12th century, is decorated with pilasters and capitals, reminiscent of ancient temples. On the triangular façade, traces of the sinopia of the frescoes of Simone Martini, removed to in the Consistory of the Papal Palace, can still be seen.

The belfry, damaged during the siege of the Palace (1405), was rebuilt without its spire. In the 17th century, the apse was restored and a baroque gallery added against the romanesque nave, considered too severe. Heavily damaged during the Revolution, the church was restored and opened for services in 1822.

In 1859, the belfry was topped by a statue of the Virgin, the aesthetics of which have sparked controversy. The parvis, encumbered by an imposing 19th-century calvary, opens onto a belvedere on the Palace Square and offers a superb partial view of the city.

Notre-Dame-des-Doms,
Papal See

THE MINT

Its richly ornamented façade contrasts with the austerity of the Papal Palace. The legate Cafarelli-Borghese reigned over the palace when vice-legate Jean-François de Bagni decided to build it in 1619. The mint takes its name from the coin minting workshop that it must have housed. Two winged gerfalcons, flanked by two eagles, watch over the Palace Square from the top of the balustrade. Just above, two angels frame a coat of arms while lions hold a profusion of sculpted fruits and vegetables in relief in their jaws. The eagle and gerfalcon are the emblem of the Borgheses, the family of the pope reigning at the time, Paul V, and his legate nephew.

The identity of the architect of this exuberant building is unknown, for the archives were destroyed during the Revolution.

Following the departure of the legation, the mint became a barracks until 1840 when the city administration moved in. Since 1860, it has housed the City Conservatory of Music.

THE SMALL PALACE

With its crenelated façade and its double row of Renaissance windows, the present museum of the Small Palace elegantly closes off the north end of the Palace Square.

Built around a cloister in 1317 by Beranger Fredol, Arnaud de Via, nephew of John XXII bought it to make it his livery. Pope Benedict XII, who had had to destroy the old bishop's palace to build the new one, acquired Arnaud de Via's residence to house the bishop. Heavily damaged by the succession of conflicts and sieges aimed at the Papal Palace, the edifice was restored in the 15th century by Bishop Alain de Coëtivy and by his successor Cardinal Giulio Della Rovere, the future pope Julius II, who transformed and beautified it to receive important guests. The gunpowder explosion at the rock of Doms in 1650 shook the foundations of the palace and its defensive tower collapsed in 1767.

Today it is an internationally renowned museum, featuring an exceptional collection of Italian paintings from the 13th to 16th centuries and some works of the Avignon school.

1   2   3

THE SAINT BENEZET BRIDGE

The construction of the original bridge remains a source of controversy today. In all likelihood, the Benezet bridge was built over the ruins of a Roman bridge, simply by adding wooden spars, and the good Benezet simply collected the funds for its completion.

Destroyed in 1226 during the siege of the city, the bridge was rebuilt in stone, 900-meters long, with 22 arches; these were supported by pilings fitted with spurs and outflows at the base to better resist the river's currents and flooding. To protect the bridge, a fort was built on the city side, and the Philippe-le-Bel tower (13th century) faced it at the other end.

In the 14th century, the construction of the new rampart encroached on one arch. Over the years, the violent waters of the Rhone caused much damage to the bridge. Despite repairs, its poor condition led its to its abandon in 1633. The restorations during the 19th century saved the four arches with can be seen today.

The chapel

The remains of the holy shepherd Benezet once laid in the lovely stone chapel on the bridge. The reconstruction of the edifice, in the 13th century, entailed the addition of one storey to the chapel due to the raising of the superstructure of the older bridge. At the end of the 14th century, a chapel dedicated to the patron saint of the Rhone sailors, Saint Nicholas, was added. Transformed again in the 15th century, a pinnacle turret and a new apse were added (1513).

A shepherd named Benezet

If the Saint Benezet bridge owes it fame to a song, its existence is owed to a young shepherd from Ardeche, who, according to legend, heard voices who instructed him to built a bridge over the Rhone at Avignon. Upon reaching the city, he was thought to be mad but he finally convinced the bishop and the people by moving, alone and effortlessly, a huge rock. Faced with this miracle, donations flowed in and the bridge was built in eight years (1177-1185). However Benezet died in 1184 before seeing his project completed. His title of saint is owed to legend and not beatification by the church. It is said that his body was intact when exhumed in 1670 from the bridge chapel, to be moved to the Celestine Church.

1 - The Bridge
2 - The Fort
3 - The Chapel
4 - Detail of the banner
of the brotherhood of Rhone
stevedores,
Museum of old Avignon

4

The Champeaux gate,
suspended keystone vault

Short Bibliography

SYLVAIN GAGNIERE
(Honorary Curator of the Papal Palace)
The Papal Palace of Avignon
Édition RMG-Papal Palace

DOMINIQUE VINGTAIN
(Curator of the Papal Palace)
Avignon. The Papal Palace
Édition Zodiaque

Dominique Paladilhe
The Popes in Avignon
Édition Perrin

Graphic design
Saluces, Avignon

Photographic credits
Henri Gaud, and RMG fund - Papal Palace
barring error or omission

ÉDITION
RMG-PALAIS DES PAPES 84000 AVIGNON
+33 (0)4 90 27 50 00
E-MAIL : rmg@palais-des-papes.com
EDITIONS GAUD 77950 MOISENAY
+33 (0)1 60 66 94 60
E-MAIL : info@editionsgaud.com

1er dépôt légal 4e trimestre 1998
retirage dépôt légal 1er trimestre 2004

3ème édition anglaise 2004
ISBN 2-84080-064-0   ISSN 1251-4454